T0149594

HOW TO TAP INTO THE ROOT WITH EFT

*Your Inner Child
Has Something to Say . . .*

ELAINE COX

BALBOA.
PRESS

A DIVISION OF HAY HOUSE

Interior Graphics/Art Credit: Troy Cox

Balboa Press books may be ordered through booksellers or by contacting:

Balboa Press
A Division of Hay House
1663 Liberty Drive
Bloomington, IN 47403
www.balboapress.com
1 (877) 407-4847

Print information available on the last page.

ISBN: 978-1-5043-7278-7 (sc)
ISBN: 978-1-5043-7280-0 (hc)
ISBN: 978-1-5043-7279-4 (e)

Library of Congress Control Number: 2017900006

Balboa Press rev. date: 01/26/2017

It is with great honor I dedicate this book in Memory of:
Tina Girard Barnstable
"Without you I would not have been led to EFT nor
would I have had a reason to write this book."
May your spirit touch the readers in the same way you
touched all of us that knew you and LOVED YOU!
Interesting Fact: My Mom, My Grand Daughter and
Tina Girard Barnstable share the same birth date.

CONTENTS

Cover and Interior Graphic / Arts Credit: TROY COX.
Prints Available: Troy Cox / elainecox351@gmail.com

CHAPTER ONE

What is EFT?

Emotional Freedom Techniques (EFT) is based on the same principles as acupuncture, but use a tapping method instead of needles.

It is believed that the imbalance of the energy system in our bodies have a profoundly negative effect on our physical and emotional health. Doctors often tell us that our symptoms are caused by stress.

Dr. Roger Callahan's first experience with EFT was in 1980. One of his patients, was suffering from frequent headaches and nightmares. She sought help from different therapists for years without much success. Dr. Callahan had been working with her for a year without making much headway.

One day, he stepped outside of the normal "boundaries"

of psychotherapy. After studying the body's energy system, he decided to tap with his fingertips under her eyes (the end point of the stomach meridian). She had complained of stomach upset and fear of water and swimming pools.

To his astonishment, she opened her eyes and immediately announced that her disturbing thoughts about water were gone. She raced down to the nearby swimming pool and started splashing water on her face. No fear. No headaches.

It all went away.....including the nightmares, and never returned. His patient is now free of her aqua phobia. Results like that are rare in the field of psychotherapy...but common with EFT.

My Introduction to EFT

EFT came in to my life in September 2009; a friend of mine was mourning the loss of her thirty-five-year-old daughter to breast cancer.

Realizing it was the one year anniversary of her daughter's passing, I was quick to accept her invitation to attend an EFT healing circle.

She shared with me that EFT was helping her deal with her grief, which seemed insurmountable at times. I could see it was making a difference for her. Not sure what EFT was, I was interested.

She had mentioned she would like to have someone to tap with. She informed me that it was a method of releasing stress by tapping on certain points on our body. She told me, the coach would be guiding us.

After watching the Coach tapping on different points with others in the group, I would be next to try. It seemed like it could be a good fit for me, since stress had become something of my specialty.

I was not feeling well. Most of the time, I was extremely exhausted, overwhelmed and angry. Many things beyond my control had just turned my world upside down. In short, I felt helpless and overwhelmed.

At the time, I was cleaning a few houses a week while my daughter attended school. I enjoyed cleaning and the sense of accomplishment I felt in putting things in order. I believed I was very good at it and could do a lot of work in the allotted time.

I now realize that I was working on adrenaline most of the time. My plan was to set a timer and work against the clock. I would push myself to exhaustion. I inevitably burned myself out many times. I would quit all the jobs, then after spending some time healing and recuperating, I would find more houses to clean, promising myself this time was going to be different. Of course, it wasn't, because I did the same thing each and every time while expecting a different result.

I would end up angrier at myself each time I replayed this insane game. I did not realize that I was harming myself at the time. I believed I was doing everything to the best of my ability. Although I did feel it was a low job in society's eyes, I also believed it worked for my family needs.

During my tapping turn, I realized how much anger and resentment I was holding in. After a few minutes of saying these things out loud, I felt an awakening of sorts. Tapping brought up a lot of other thoughts I had not been aware I even felt.

The coach asked me if I liked feeling this way. I replied back by saying, "Of course I don't want to feel like this." I was making myself sick. I was not only emotionally up set I was having reactions to the cleaners, which no doubt filled my body with toxins.

I felt a complete shift, not only in my body but also my thinking. Feelings of worthlessness also surfaced.

The coach asked me whether I had felt that anger and worthlessness as a child. Thinking back I knew immediately where it came from and why I felt this way.

Just understanding its source shifted my energy and thoughts. It was amazing to me how much better I felt. The other participants in the healing circle witnessed my transformation.

My mind was clear. I made a decision right then and there. I would not be cleaning houses anymore. I let go of all my clients at once.

Imagine shifting all that blocked energy in such a short time. Feeling clear headed and having a new perspective, enabling me to make a good decision quickly.

I felt the release; I was hooked wanting more of this feeling. I certainly did not want to go back to the way I felt entering this room. I now felt calm, sure of myself, relieved. I realized that EFT would be very beneficial to me.

I began to attend weekly healing circles and one-on-one sessions with an EFT coach. My friend and I set aside time to tap together. It was like peeling back an onion; we were clearing emotional stress one layer at a time.

Even though there are many levels to an issue, it may take a few EFT sessions to get to the root. Your subconscious will only release what you are ready to hear. Be kind to yourself. Working through your issues at your own pace will bring wonderful results.

Sentences starting with "even though" or "what if" need to be repeated three times... Even though I feel.... I accept myself....I deeply and completely accept this issue...I deeply and completely love and accept myself. What if...these two words can be used to move you, from where you are in your thinking to where you choose to go, opening the door to a new idea? *Example*: what if I could get that or do what I really want to do?

Adding your own words to fill in the blanks, as you become more familiar with EFT will give you a sense of power.

And so my personal journey began, I felt immediate results on many different emotional levels. I began trying it out on my husband, friends and family members. To my surprise, they felt their energy shift too.

My dream to become an EFT coach was born. I began reading books on the topic. I signed up online for the Gary Craig course.

This past year I took a workshop on line by Nick and Jessica Ortner called *Seven Weeks to Financial Success and Personal Fulfillment*. One statement that resonated with me from that program was "Put Yourself Out There." Hence! I made a conscious decision to write this book. Over the years I have coached countless friends, family members and clients.

Emotional Freedom Techniques

EFT releases blocked energy causing emotional suffering. We store these emotions in different parts of our bodies, which will create physical pain.

Long standing emotional pain can lead to serious physical issues. Tapping out the emotional pain clears the energy system, allowing physical healing as well as emotional healing.

This method is 100% physician approved. Visit www. emofree.com to access the manual by Gary Craig.

EFT works on all kinds of issues:

Pain Relief
Fears and Phobias
Allergies
Trauma
Depression
Anxiety
PTSD
Disease

Tapping Points

EB = Beginning of the Eye Brow

SE = Side of the Eye

UE = Under Eye

UN = Under the Nose

CH = Chin

CB = Beginning of the Collarbone

UA = Under the Arm

BN = Below the Nipple

TH = Thumb (side of the thumb at the base of the nail)

IF = Index finger (side of the nail)

MF = Middle Finger (side of the nail)

BF = Baby Finger (side of the nail)

KC = Karate Chop (fleshy side of your hand between the little finger and the base of wrist).

Listed above are the basic points to tap on. For now we are going to be using the side of the hand, the Karate Chop point.

I will ask you to tap lightly on the Karate Chop point, whenever you feel a disruption in your energy system, while reading the stories or scripts I have provided.

Children respond well to tapping on the side of their fingers, at the base of the nail. These points are called magic buttons. Many children suffer from anxiety, which is now being recognized as a real issue. Energy is everywhere, both positive and negative. Children are like sponges soaking it all up.

They are very receptive to learning and being taught how to think and feel, in all areas of their lives. Unlike adults, they have not learned to filter or doubt what they are told.

Children feel what we feel, have trouble articulating what they want to say. They become frustrated and act out in ways we don't understand.

It is important to work with parents first, before tapping with their children. A child will feel immediate results when the parents around them release their anxiety. Their child will feel the shift, which allows anxiety to vanish quickly in them. They feel they are safe.

Clear yourself first by releasing your own stress around an issue. After you have cleared your blocks, it is time to start tapping lightly on the top of your child's head or on their fingers at the side of the nail. Often as you clear your own stress, your child will be releasing along with you. Releasing energy works wonders this way.

CHAPTER TWO

Self-Awareness is the Key

Most of us just rush through our days with little time to do the things we have to do, without having time to stop and think about how we do them. The roller coaster of life gets in the way. At the end of the day, we are exhausted and still have a to-do list a mile long.

We fall into bed feeling unfulfilled, frustrated, and often angry at someone in our life for not helping us out or for hurting us.

Still reeling from what was said or done, we sense another sleepless night on the horizon. Add to that all the bills that need paying and laundry stacked to the ceiling. The kids have to be taken to many after-school activities. They seem grumpy lately as well.

Sound familiar? Sad, isn't it.

No wonder so many people are suffering from depression and anxiety having to rely on anti-depressants to get through the day.

We can continue on this path and find ourselves adding to our ailments. How many of us live this way? I have felt like this many times. If only there were two of me I would be able to stay on top of the demands. I really hope you don't hold that belief.

The first thing I want you to do is ask yourself if any of this rings true. If not, then put this book down and continue on your path, or go fishing like my Dad did. If it does ring true, please be kind to yourself.

Admitting to yourself you would like to hear more about the possibility of changing things will open you up to self-awareness.

EFT Script

The EFT Script below is made up of key components to help you understand how you can begin your tapping process. The words "even though" help you identify that you have an issue you want to look at. It is called the set up statement.

Even though I have never thought of self-awareness before, I realize that I do feel overwhelmed at times. Even though I have no idea what reading this script is supposed to do, I am a good person with lots of great qualities and I am willing to be open to the possibility of change.

What if, I hear one thing that helps me? I could work on that. I know I find myself getting angry quickly. It makes me feel out of control.

Below, you will find a few questions to ask yourself. Thinking about each question and answering honestly will open your mind to new insights.

When in your life do you remember getting angry and out of control?

Who made you angry?

Where were you?

Were you alone with the person or were others around?

Can you close your eyes and envision yourself and the other person(s)?

How old were you?

What did you do?

After answering these questions, you will find you have some answers. We all have the answers in us. All we need to do is stop, reflect and tap into our subconscious.

Tap on the Karate Chop point (side of your hand).

Even though I was very angry, I accept myself anyway. Even though I was very angry, I accept myself anyway. Even though I was very angry, I accept myself anyway. I deeply and completely accept what I did and said.

I was ___ years old. I was only ____ years old.

I can see I didn't really know any other way to act. I was only doing what I knew and I accept myself. This is the way we act in my family. Everyone does it. At least that is what I always believed until now.

What if, that is why I am carrying all this anger today? Maybe it doesn't just go away. I was ___ years old and now I am ____ years old. Is this my pattern?

Our subconscious brains are wired to remember the way we reacted the first time we did something. For example, if your first memory of being angry and out of control is when you were eight years old, that is what will come to the surface. Your subconscious has been holding that for all these years, and when you get angry, you are still reacting from that eight-year-old child inside you.

This is where you can assure the little girl inside that it is okay. Tell her you forgive her, you understand how she felt and why she acted out of control.

* Always use your own words and gender of course, as I used female in this example.

Once you come to the revelation of the reason you were angry and felt out of control and the timeline, you will probably feel many shifts in your energy.

The farther back you can go in your memory, the greater the understanding you will have. Looking at it from this age gives you a totally different perspective.

Self-awareness will help you change your understanding and enable you to see the situation from another angle.

Basics of Our Beliefs

We all hold a set of beliefs close to our heart. We learned these things as children growing up. Our parents told us what to do and why to do it. Teachers, mentors, and spiritual leaders in our lives all contributed to what we believe today.

These personal beliefs are what we all live by, and base our decisions on. We just do what we always did. It is the writing on our wall. More often than not, we never question if these things are still true for us today in our adult life.

Think about it for minute. Look at the writing on your wall. Some of it holds true. Some may have no value for you today. Which beliefs do you want to disregard?

What if you could change one or two of these so-called truths? Which one would you change? You may have been told that you cannot do something in front of grandma. Every time you see grandma today you remember that rule.

Or that it is not safe to talk to strangers. This could have become a deep-rooted fear in you, and you are now hesitant to work in sales or make new connections.

EFT can help you understand that your issue today may be

attached to something you were told as a child, which could be keeping you stuck at whatever age you learned it.

By tapping out the fear of talking to strangers and assuring your inner child that she is safe. Explain to her, you are an adult now, and making adult decisions. You will feel a release of blocked energy and have the understanding of why you felt the way you did.

There is no doubt that this fear has also affected some part of your body. You are storing it somewhere. Our stomachs are famous for welcoming fear. You can be sure over the years it will show up as an ulcer or digestive problems.

Changing your belief to fit the adult you have become, will clear away all the anger and fear around an issue, the aliment will likely disappear as well.

House of Possibilities

As you walk through this house, you notice there are a lot of choices. More choices than you ever imagined. Something jumps out at you, your heart quickens. You feel light and energized, realizing how you have always been interested in that.

Then you hear that critical little voice in your head that says you cannot do that or have that. You are too old, or much too young. Do you really think you are smart enough? You will need a university degree for that. No one in our family has ever done that before, so what makes you think you can?

These negative, limiting thoughts put up blocks in your

energy system. Keeping you stuck at the age you learned or heard these things. We often never give it another thought. It becomes the writing on our wall.

This can be a regular day for a lot of people. Yet a lot of people move forward and accept these thoughts with such ease. Very few people stop to wonder, *why not?* Or *what if?*

Again, the adults in our life told us these things or perhaps we overheard someone say them. We remember these words in our subconscious, and they can stop us from reaching our goals.

As we become aware that this is happening, it opens a door, giving us a better understanding as to why we may be stuck.

Be open to the possibilities in every area of your life. Tap on it and see what comes up. Once you see what the block really is you will be able to move forward instantly.

Drawing Parallels

It is like connecting the dots. Whatever the issue, it brings self awareness and understanding to how we react exactly the same way every time it comes up. It helps to show you what your patterns are with each emotional issue. You can then make a conscious choice if you want to keep or change something to get the outcome you desire.

If you are not making as much money as you would like to be making or can't seem to hold on to much money, you may feel worthless. Going back to the first time you felt this feeling of worthlessness over not having enough. You may find when you were ten, you lost some money and you even forgot you lost it until now. You had no idea it had anything to do with today's issue.

This is where you developed your emotions about money. Are you making money decisions based on that past emotion? Are you feeling the same today as you did that day many years ago?

Connect the dots and tap out the old pattern. Are you afraid you will lose money? Create a new thought. Allow yourself to accept money, hold on to money to have money flow to you.

Say this out loud. Even though I have had issues with money in the past, I am great with money today. I am allowing money to flow to me. I always have all the money I need when I need it. I am open to creating more money.

What Role do You Play in this Movie we call Life?

We all play a role. We have been taught how to act by everyone —parents, grandparents, teachers, older siblings and society. We try to play by the rules they set or act according to the way they think things should be done.

After all, they know best, so it must be the truth. It is the way it is done, period. We live our life playing this role to the best of our ability. Often we don't ever question who set the rules and decided the roles.

Who told you how to act? Did it seem fair? Do you ever wonder or question these ideas or beliefs? Who got angry if you didn't act as you were told? What happened? What was your reaction to the situation? Did you fill the role? Personally, I use to play the people-pleaser role very well. It was all I knew.

What does it feel like today now that you are an adult? Do these things still ring true? Are these still your beliefs?

Some roles are extremely hard to fill. You may feel you are not cut out for a certain role, yet you try and fail and get frustrated. React, get in trouble, feel overwhelmed, and anxiety begins to unfold. No one will listen to you. It feels like no one hears you, but you still try to please everyone.

You feel like you have no control over anything in your life. Yet you keep doing the same things over and over. Even as despair overtakes you, you keep assuring yourself that this is what you want. This is the way it is supposed to be. You just have to get better at it.

Some roles are easy, and everything flows well. You feel supported, fulfilled and understood. Everything you touch works out really well. You have a really good day and wonder why it can't always be like that. How would that feel?

I spent many years in the first role. I didn't know it was as bad as it was. I believed I was doing something wrong if I couldn't keep up to all the demands. Sometime I would neglect one thing to jump into another so I could feel successful, only to have yet another person to please.

Then I would blame it on them and beat myself up because I was not good enough. I never realized I was doing it to myself.

Anytime one family member is affected by any kind of emotional discomfort, it will move through the generations, with emotional pain being sent up or down the family tree. It will be wide spread sending energy to siblings and friends. Humans care about one another; we feel each other's energy. If they hurt, we hurt.

We are happy when our parents are well, when our children are happy, when things are good for all of us.

Note: EFT works over the telephone, tapping on your own or in a group. Even tapping for others works.

CHAPTER
THREE

Patient Recovering from Colon Cancer Surgery

It was early afternoon in May, 2012. The sun was shining as I arrived at the hospital to visit someone special to me who was recovering from colon cancer surgery.

It was day eleven after the surgery and she still had not had a bowel movement, which meant things were not going well.

As I entered the hospital room, I stopped in my tracks. Seeing the shape she was in startled me. I immediately knew something bad was happening.

A nurse was with her and I could see she was trying to get her to lay flat. She was in extreme pain. Sitting in an upright fetal position, knees drawn up to her chest, clasping her hands together, beads of sweat periling on her forehead. Through gasps and groans, she managed to tell me that there was a twist or block and she needed more surgery.

The nurse in attendance stepped back, stating, "We need her to lay flat. She will not cooperate; we have been doing everything possible, but we cannot get her to budge." On her way out, she said she was going to get some help and would be right back.

I knew we needed to start tapping. We had tapped together before. Knowing she responded well in the past, I knew if anything would help, it would be this wonderful technique.

Her entire body felt frozen in place, it was like touching a statue. She told me she was scared, and pretty certain that this was the end for her. Her forehead was burning up, yet her feet were freezing.

I reached out to take her hand in mine and immediately felt that she was literally hanging on for dear life. She said, "God has forsaken me."

When I touched her hand with mine, it was cold and it felt stiff and hard, like cement. I started tapping on the Karate Chop point for a couple of minutes, moving to the top of her head. I asked her to repeat after me. Even though I am scared to death and this pain is crippling, I want to get better. Even though I am in intense pain, I want to get better. Even though it is so severe, I can't move I want this to stop. I do not want to die.

She whispered: "I am really scared God is not answering me." I ran cold water on a cloth and applied it to her forehead and continued to tap on the Karate Chop point.

The nurse returned, seeing I was in the middle of something, hearing she was repeating my words out loud. The Nurse was surprised she was even cooperating.

I asked for a hot towel for her feet and she brought two, telling me where I could find more. The Nurse said, "I don't know what you are doing, but this is the best she has been all day. If there is anything you need, ring the buzzer and take as many towels as you need."

I began to wrap her feet in the hot towels. She allowed me to move her foot, one at a time, ever so slightly. I was able to wrap each of them.

She repeated after me. Even though my feet are freezing, the warm towels feel good. She told me how she had been unable to move because of the pain and the nurses were getting upset with her. It was the worst pain she had ever experienced.

I began to tap above her eyebrow, side of her eye, under her eye, above her lip, and on her chin. It was impossible to get her to move her head. After a few more rounds of tapping and asking her to relax her jaw, neck, head, spine, and shoulders, I saw that she was starting to thaw.

Her bed was in an upright position with pillows behind her head; she finally let her head release and laid it back on the pillow, still in an upright position.

We had more work to do. I asked if I could take her hand, if she thought I could move it just a little bit, to get a better position. As I tapped on the side of her hand, the tension started to release in her fingers, I was able to feel life coming back into her cement-like hands.

I asked her to repeat after me. Even though I thought I could not move, I did move a little bit. My head is resting on the pillow and I can move my fingers a little.

Even though I am still holding on tightly, with my arms to my chest, I feel like I am holding on for dear life. Maybe I can let go a little bit more. At least I am willing to try.

As I tapped more on the Karate Chop point, I felt her release at the elbow and now I was holding her hand that was warming up to the possibility of healing. The pain was still there. She accepted it as it was, realizing she did have some control over some parts of her body, even if it was just to relax them. She allowed herself to release some of her fear.

With more rounds of tapping and more hot towels for her feet and cold cloths for her forehead, she was able to let me move her feet a little farther from her chest. It was much easier now.

Releasing some more, she started to feel that she did have support from God. He was in fact with her now. I asked her if she could hear what He was saying. She said, "He is saying I will be okay." With that, her feet slid down the bed, her legs stretched out straight. She whispered to herself, "Thank You. Thank You. Thank You. Amen."

The energy was flowing. I continued tapping on different points while she said some prayers.

The nurse stuck her head in the door and could not believe

her eyes. She just backed away and left us to do what we do best. Tap.

Feeling some better she said, "Maybe you can let the bed down now." More and more nurses peeked through the open door, astonished to see how well she was responding to this thing I was doing.

We tapped on the pain. Of course, it was severe, black and haunting, but she didn't feel as afraid as she was when I came in to visit. As she released and let go of all the fear, the pain subsided. She laid flat in bed with her eyes shut, totally limp.

She transformed from a frozen statue to rag doll in less than one hour. She was sound asleep.

It always amazes me every time I witness EFT at work. The transformation was beyond anything I could ever have imagined, had I not experienced it firsthand. I was confident yet again that EFT can work miracles.

Things Happen for a Reason

So many things were in play that day beyond any of our understanding. I was brought to the hospital at the right time to do this for her. Even though she had been in the hospital for eleven days, this was only my second visit. It had been eleven days of making phone calls to see if she had that first bowel movement.

At about 7:30 pm the evening of my visit, she called to tell me she was not having surgery. The block or twist had corrected itself and her bowels were working. She said she was exhausted but feeling a lot better.

EFT was the tool that helped her release her pain, fear, and anguish. By allowing herself to be led with this incredible tool, she allowed herself to heal.

In the months that followed, we often tapped before her chemotherapy and radiation treatments. She would ask her body to accept the treatment in the exact area it was needed, to kill the cancer and to protect all other cells, organs and parts of her body that were helping her heal herself.

She has now been cancer-free or in remission as the experts say for four years.

She often talks about that day and wonders what would have happened to her had I not come to visit, What if I never tried EFT with her? She goes as far as saying she doesn't believe she would be with us today.

No one knows what would have happened or whether she would have had to have corrective surgery. What we do know is things happen for a reason. The people we need will be sent to us. Yet, she is the one who had the power to come back from that dark scary place.

To this day, she still says I saved her life. What I do know, without a doubt, EFT did make an incredible difference.

I was only the Coach leading her that day. Although it feels good to hear her say that, I know that I alone can't save lives.

Each person has to want to live, has to have the desire to

heal, to be open to the possibility of doing the inner work in order to make the changes needed to heal.

If I had the power to save lives, there would be a lot more of our loved ones with us today.

She was the one open to the possibility of healing herself. She was the one that did the inside job, the difficult job. No one can do it for us.

We create all the experiences in our lives, the good, the bad, and the ugly. Yet we refuse to believe that we create the bad or the ugly. We don't even allow ourselves to accept the credit when we do the good in our lives.

What if we were open to the understanding of how we created the cancer in the first place? How would that change the outcome?

According to Louise Hay, author of *You Can Heal your Life*, the emotion behind cancer is: Long with standing anger.

We hear all the time that stress causes so many diseases. Maybe it would be wise to take a look at this theory. What if we could release the anger before it creates the disease?

CHAPTER FOUR

My Story

I am very happy to have created this opportunity for myself to go spend a week alone in the mountains with an ocean view.

It is a beautiful little town, very quiet place that lends itself to thinking, meditating, writing and exploring. The energy here is so uplifting.

It is set on an inlet; the calm ocean and pristine mountains encircle the town. Trees tower over my head as I walk along pebbled paths. I look up in wonder at the soaring eagles flying over the water, hoping to catch a jumping fish.

The air is crisp, fresh from last night's rain. The rising sun was burning off the fog, bringing into view bright blue skies.

Soon the sun will be shining down on this little town and

all the people that live here. I am extremely excited to have the sun shine down on me, seeping deep into my soul, helping me with my personal journey.

I always knew I had it in me to write a book and I often contemplated the idea. It would be exciting to write. I lived to write.

I have binders filled with lined paper, expressing my thoughts of the day, week or month. I would find many thoughts on those pages. I was writing about things that made me happy, sad and angry. In the words, I would find answers.

I learned over time to find messages in my writing, to find healing. Often, when I felt stuck on some level, I could see the patterns that needed breaking, yet fear held me back.

My fear of saying "no" to someone was like being strangled. I felt it was better to do things I didn't want to do for people I didn't want to help than the pain and guilt I would suffer by saying no.

I believed if I just did it, I could rest. I lived my entire life with this thought process. However, every time I did one thing, it seemed to have a ten step follow up. More came, more of the same, because that is what I was creating.

I attracted more of these kinds of situations. I created them in all areas of my life.

By working with EFT and recreating my thought patterns, I am pleased to say today is the day I write the story and lay the past to rest.

This week has been very healing for me and I have released a lot of blocks. If I would have written this story five years ago,

I can honestly say it would have been from a very different perspective. It may have come from a place of disappointment, resentment, embarrassment, fear or anger.

Most of these feeling were directed at me, how I wrecked our family. Yet I am torn by the fact that if it were not for the turmoil, I would not be here today.

Most of my life I left these issues dormant in my subconscious, not realizing that this was the very reason I was filled with anxiety. Carrying this burden deep in my subconscious for more than forty years is a long time.

EFT helped me come to terms with many different facets of my upbringing. Understanding why I felt the way I did as a child and why I reacted to issues in all areas of my life with emotional upheaval.

My intention is to write my book about EFT while telling my story and how I went from where I was physically and emotionally to where I am today. I chose EFT as my tool to tap into the root of my issues. Understanding the why behind my issues makes it much easier for me to release fear or anger.

My parents were married Oct, 1938. They lived on an acreage. I was the sixth of seven children, with older siblings ranging in ages from eight to eighteen. We lived a half mile from the country store. My Dad and his brother owned and operated the store and post office.

As the due date of my birth approached, my mom travelled by train to the nearby town to be close to the hospital. She stayed with a relative as she awaited my arrival. After a ten day stay in the hospital, Mom and I were released.

Waiting to accompany us home were my older sister's and my Dad. One of my sisters said it was a special day for her, riding the train for the first time and a new baby.

The aftermath of childbirth can be a very emotional time for any new mother. My mother was certainly not without emotional pain. I had many older siblings, and I am sure it was difficult for my mother to give us all care the and attention we required.

I remember Mom telling me stories of how hard it was on her. She even said she had a nervous breakdown after I was born. I wondered where all the older siblings were and why she felt she had no support. She said they moved to the city to work and only came home on weekends.

She told me about the wonderful neighbours who lived half a mile away on a farm. She says they often helped her and gave support when no one else would.

As I got older I saw these people were in fact good to her. I called the man by his name and his wife Grandma. Mom did work for them and helped them with farming and haying.

Even as a young child I could feel the tension and anxiety swirling all around me. As I got older, I could see Mom was very unhappy and never seemed to get what she needed or wanted.

When I was sick, as I often was, she would call upon this neighbouring family. They came to help whenever she needed them. Dad worked at the store six days a week and was unable to leave during the day, except for the lunch hour.

These neighbors also had a son Mac, who was twenty-two when I was born. He spent a lot of time at our house. He lived with his parent's on the farm. He was slightly older than my siblings. It was a busy household to say the least.

There were no phones in those days. Finding ways to communicate was a challenge. When Mom needed help, she would turn on a light on the front of our house. The neighbor or his son Mac would see the light and know they were needed. One of them would walk the half-mile to help her with me.

I remember Mac was called upon a lot. He generously rushed to her aide to see what she needed. Usually, she needed help with me, especially if I had an ear ache or tonsillitis.

Upon his arrival she would tell him to take me and see if he could do something with me, since she was at her wits end with my crying and had tried everything to calm me.

Even though Mom said she did everything for me, I honestly don't ever remember her holding me or trying to comfort me. I was too heavy and hurt her knees or was in the way of her smoking or whatever she was doing. She loved to do fancy work, as she called it knitting, crocheting and embroidering

Mac would calm me down in five minutes, doing what was needed for ear aches. I would fall asleep in his arms. Then Dad would bring cold medicine, juice and fruit home at lunch time to help me feel better.

I learned early on that if I wanted attention from mom, I could get it by doing something for her. Whenever I brought her something or picked up my toys she would tell me that I was a good girl and that makes mommy happy.

I was always eager to please her and see her happy. Thus began my life-long journey of people pleasing.

It seemed like everyone needed my help and I believe I was able to make a lot of people happy. I helped every single person I came in contact with, even the ones that didn't ask. I prided myself on doing my best and giving one hundred and ten percent.

My Schooling

I attended a small one-room country school. It was new construction, with a hallway, a boot room, a storage room for supplies and a wash stand with the water cooler.

The school was located on one acre of land, a mile away from our home. The school had a blue exterior; large windows along one wall and a big porch on the front.

There was a well with a hand pump, from which older student's hauled water into the school. One student held the bucket while a couple of other students pumped the steel handle. There was a hook for the pail to hang on if we chose to use it. We always got wet packing in the water.

The ball diamond was at the back of the property. A girls' wash room, an outhouse, was on the west side of the acreage while the boys' washroom was on the east side. We had a big swing set as well as a teeter totter.

Student body consisted of around thirty boys and girls, from grade one to eight during my first year of school.

When I was in grade two, the county decided to move grade seven and eight to a larger school in a nearby town. My teacher taught all six grades for the six years I attended school there.

I was an anxious, nervous child, and school only added to my anxiety. At age nine, in grade four, I was plagued with stomach problems daily.

It wasn't that I didn't like school. It was more about fear of getting into trouble from the teacher. The rules were much harsher in those days. If we got three spelling words wrong, we lined up to get the strap. If we didn't sit up straight, we could get our ears pulled. Often, other classmates were hit with a yard stick or a pointer for various reasons.

Even though none of these things happened to me, I was afraid I would be next. My anxiety grew with each passing day, creating more health issues.

Mom took me for many doctor appointments and tests at the small town hospital. They told her it was just nerves, which I suppose equates to anxiety today. It was decided I needed to be kept at home for the rest of grade four, which was two months followed by summer holidays.

During that time, I was taken to a doctor in a bigger city. I spent a week at the hospital, alone and away from my parents who could only visit for a couple of hours during visiting hours; this only added to my fear of being alone. From that bout of testing, it was decided I needed to be put on a diet free of gluten.

Having to stay away from school created more inner turmoil. Staying at home was stressful enough without all the appointments and tests. Mom was worried about my health.

The gap between grades four and five was huge. I had missed a lot of learning time and social time with friends.

Being in a small school setting does not leave a lot of choice of friends. I wanted to play with my cousin, but she wanted to play with a girl two years older than her. I was far too young. "Get lost," are two words I heard a lot in school. Mom tells me that she would go to the school occasionally to set things straight.

Sometimes my teacher would stop by the house to talk to Mom. They were always quarrelling. Mac was also taught by her so he had issues of his own regarding her. His anger was apparent. All I wanted was for them all to get along.

One day during my two-month stay at home, I had walked the half mile to the store to see Dad.

On my way home, who should come down the road as I was strolling along? My teacher! I knew I was not to let her see me out and about. I panicked as soon as I saw her vehicle coming, I ran as fast as I could to get to my house before she caught me. She had the window open yelling at me, "Stop! Get in the car now!"

I could feel the cramping pain in my legs, the burning sensation in my lungs and the tears flowing down my cheeks. It was the sheerest terror I ever felt. Talk about being chased by the tiger; she was the tiger after me for sure. She was shouting that I was not sick and was just playing my Mom.

I arrived at my door with her in tow. Dread grew in my gut, knowing that there was going to be a huge battle between Mom and her.

Then when Mac got a hold of her there would be more. He loved a chance to go to battle with this teacher. It gave him a chance to yet again release his frustration from childhood.

He would go into a rage. She would finally leave, and Mom and Mac would declare they were taking the matter to the school board. I was sick of the countless meetings with school officials and doctor appointments.

All I wanted was to get better so I could make them all happy. Yet the fear of that teacher and the dysfunctional atmosphere in the classroom did not help the healing process.

Wanting to be good, I pushed down more of the pain, anger and hurt. I sat on pins and needles at school all day and then when I went home, the tension was there too, causing me to develop all the emotional distress.

My grade six class was made up of me and one male student. I am not sure if I was top of the class or bottom for grades. It would be my last year there. It seemed that everywhere I turned, it was scary.

In grade seven, we were integrated into a school in the nearby town housing four classrooms of grade seven students.

I knew one girl that attended that school, thinking she would be happy I was in her class, didn't work out the way I thought it was going to. I found I was in the same position as in elementary.

She too already had friends. It took me a long time to make real friends. I soon discovered, if I did exactly what a friend wanted me to do and agreed with them on every level, I could make some head way.

That is when my people pleasing nature became solidified. Just after Christmas in grade eight, I became friends with a girl from one of the other classes. She and I become lifelong friends. We spent a lot of time together. I would go to her house to eat my lunch and spend the night often as she lived in town.

Leaving home after finishing school, we shared an apartment together, we both for filled our dream of working in an office.

Two years after graduation we were married one week apart. She was my maid of honor and I was her bridesmaid. I was excited to move to the big city.

Mac Move In

Soon after Mac's father passed away, his mother moved out, leaving him with the farm. He lived there a few months, finding it impossible to fix up the dilapidated house.

In the summer, he coached the teens' softball team, which my brother was a part of. My brother was an amazing pitcher and we loved going to his games.

Mac worked building roads for the local county, operating

heavy equipment. The farm work was busy year round, with haying, harvesting crops, and tending to the livestock.

After dinner one night as Dad was reading the news paper in the living room, Mom asked my sister and me if we would like to have Mac move in and live with us. I was excited because he always spent time with us. He played the guitar and sang to me. He was fun.

Mom told us to go ask Dad if Mac could live with us. There we were doing her dirty work.

Dad looked over the newspaper with a scowl on his face, thinking for a couple of minutes. He answered, "Whatever your mother wants." I was eight years old when Mac moved into our home as a boarder.

Dad worked all the time, delivering groceries in the evenings and going fishing on Sundays.

One Sunday evening when I was sixteen years old, my sister returned home after visiting one of our older sisters. I was upstairs, reading quietly. I heard her slam the front door and stomp up the stairs. I could feel the house shake. Running to see what all the commotion was, I came face-to-face with her. Standing there, out of breath, she announced that I was Mac's kid. Turns out my older sister's husband had told her that Mac was my father.

I felt like I had been punched in the gut. What? Who said that? It couldn't be! Dad was my father! How could the boarder be my father? That would have made him twenty-two when I was born.

I knew Mom had been thirty-six and Dad forty-seven upon my birth. My head was spinning, yet I did not believe it.

How could I have lived my life for sixteen years and not known this? It had to be a lie, or maybe a joke. I was burning up with questions, but I never questioned anyone about this.

I just let it be. My sister wanted me to talk to Mom. I never saw any reason to ask because Mom just told her to believe whatever she wanted to believe. I guess I was afraid I would make her angry.

Even though I was terribly distraught, I managed once again to pull myself together and move on, thinking that whatever the lie or truth is, it is how I came to be.

I remembered one time, in grade nine my friend came to stay the night after school. She said, "You look way more like Mac than your dad." When I told Mac what she had said, He just replied, "I don't know why she would think that."

I thought it was because we both had blue eyes, but I dismissed what my friend said and didn't think anything of it.

Mom always said there were a lot of stories about her and if we heard any, they were all lies. We were to make up our own mind about what we wanted to believe. As silly as that sounds, that is exactly what I did. Dad was my Dad. End of story.

Three years later, while I was planning my wedding, the topic of who would walk me down the aisle came up for discussion. Mom said it could be anyone I want. It didn't have to be Dad.

Well who could it be? I thought that to be the most absurd thing I ever heard. What did she think? I certainly wasn't having one of my brothers walk me down the aisle. Was I supposed to ask Mac, the boarder?

Dad walked me down the aisle, while Mac drove me and the bridesmaids to church. Mac walked Mom down the aisle ahead of Dad and Me.

Even though my sister had told me Mac was my real father, this wasn't confirmed by either Mac or my Mother. I certainly wasn't going to ask Dad anything about it. That would hurt his feelings. I felt I would be dishonoring him.

Mac suffered a heart attack at age fifty. We were allowed in the hospital intensive care unit, I though because we were the closest thing he had to family.

I mentioned to him that we were lucky to be let in to see him. Not to worry, he told the nurses that my sister and I were his daughters. I laughed it off and told him it is not good to lie.

That line could have open up conversation, another chance for me to talk about it. I again let the ball drop.

A few times over the years, I think he tried to tell me in his own way. I guess I was not ready to deal with this issue, and as I said earlier, Dad was my Dad, no matter what. No one had come clean yet, so I held true to my belief.

Mac came home from the hospital knowing things were not good, but he played it down to keep us from worrying. Almost two months later, he suffered a major heart attack and died.

He had told me how the doctor had shown him how fast he would die when the time came. The doctor took a quarter, holding it at chest level. He told Mac, "It will be this quick.

When the quarter hits the floor, you will be gone." Then he dropped the coin on his office floor.

I did not like hearing that. I pushed that knowledge into that secret place with all the other stuff I didn't want to hear, hidden deep in my subconscious.

In the months before his death, Mac became distant and started staying out late. He was not listening to the doctor's orders. His actions created a lot of stress for my Mom.

His passing was somewhat of a shock; as he had just received a letter with the results from a stress test stating he could return to work in two months.

We all had been relieved when the letter came, thinking that things were looking good. But now he was gone.

The story of his death was another event shrouded in mystery. Apparently he and a friend were at the home of some newly divorced woman they knew.

There was a gathering and a fight allegedly broke out between him and this woman's friend.

He was said to have been found slumped over the steering wheel of his truck, with his heart medication all over the dash of his truck. Evidently showing he tried to get to his pills.

There were many tracks in the snow, indicating he had been spinning the truck in circles.

I wanted answers. For once in my life, I wanted to know the truth. Did I get it? I don't believe I did. More cover ups. More lies.

If I was really his daughter, I would have been entitled to

the talk to the police which I wanted to do. My mother told me to leave things alone; nothing would bring him back.

The morning of after his death, Mom called early to give me the news. I rushed to my family home to be with her.

Mac's brother had already came and gone. He was prepared to take care of the estate. He asked for the will. To everyone's surprise, no will was found.

Mac had known he was not well. He owned a farm as well as other assets, so it seemed strange that he hadn't prepared at all for his death.

Mom claimed she did not have his will, we all thought he may have trusted or appointed a friend as executor. No will ever surfaced. His estate was placed in the hands of a Lawyer.

In the event that there is no will, and he didn't have family of his own, his estate would be divided equally between his between his four siblings.

The land was owned by his parents; it seemed logical to me that it would go to his siblings.

Mom was upset though. She thought she would have been the beneficiary, because she had been his partner for all these years and gave the best years of her life to him.

It was obvious that she was distraught and angry. After everything she did, how could she not be left his estate?

Knowing that I was in fact his child created more stress for her. Even though she knew I was entitled to this estate since I was his biological daughter, she had lied on my birth certificate, which stated that her husband was my father.

She stuck with the story that there was no will. What a tangled web Mom wove. She was also beside herself with anger that Mac's brother jumped to the plate before she had time to even think.

Because he had died at a friend's place, the police were involved and an autopsy was performed.

Even though there had been a fight between him and this woman's friend, the autopsy states he died of a major heart attack according to Mom.

His funeral went off without a hitch.

Yet, there was something unsettling about it all. He was fairly young and the circumstances around his death left a lot of unanswered questions.

It was always understood by everyone in the family, as well as friends, that I, or "Baby," as he called me, was weak. Don't want to upset her, the fragile little thing. If anyone said anything to me, Mac jumped down their throat and coddled me.

There were a lot of snide remarks from a lot of people. I really didn't understand why he got so angry until I was older and knew what the words meant.

He was overprotective of me and smothered me with love, which, if I would have known he was my real father, I would have cherished.

Since it was just hear say, unsure of the fact for a long time, I did pull away from some of his love. It seemed too misplaced at times. I now realize where I learned to block love. Looking back now, I always knew he was in my court and had my back against the world.

Mom did finally come clean and admit to me after Mac's death that she had lied all these years to protect him. She didn't want Dad to hurt him.

She told me that since I was his daughter, I could go to the lawyer and state my case, which would entitle me to his estate.

I refused. I had lived this much of my life with Dad being my father; I could not dishonor him.

Besides, the farm was owned by Mac's parents in the first place. It seemed right that it would go to his sibling. I left it at that and went home.

The following week, Mom revealed a new twist to the story. She told me that my younger sister was also his child.

The only time I had ever heard someone say she was his child, was when Mac stated it the night of his heart attack, when he was in intensive care.

Like I said, I thought he was just making something up so nurses would let us in to see him. He did treat me as a daughter.

My younger sister was strong and independent, not scared of anything according to Mom. She was willing to do what Mom suggested, go to the lawyer I could just go with her and see what could be done.

My sister and her husband had their mobile home on Mac's farm, where they had resided since getting married.

We both visited the lawyer, who told us that if we could prove we were Mac's biological daughters, he would present our case to Mac's siblings.

Since our birth certificates did not name him, we would need to obtain letters from people in the neighbor hood stating this to be true.

Mom took charge of this. She went to six of Mac's friends asking for their help. She collected the letters.

It was hard for me to understand why all of a sudden she had confessed that my sister was also his daughter when it had never been clearly stated before.

In fact, he wasn't very nice to her, if she was his child. He would cuddle me and put his foot up to her belly to keep her from coming close to us. He would fly off the handle at her and was always scolding her for one thing or another.

Yet, when she was older he had basically arranged her marriage to a young man he worked with.

Mac and his co-worker were thinking of buying a couple gravel trucks together. That plan never materialized.

However; my sister and Mac's co-worker were married three months later. Mac was quick to suggest they move his co-worker's mobile home to his farm.

During those next three months, my sister finished high school at the end of June and was married long week end in July 1976. In the eight years that followed they were busy raising their two beautiful little girls on the farm.

Mac's death would forever change their lives. The letters

were sent to the lawyers. Mac's siblings were told of this turn of events.

I am sure they were perplexed and did their own investigating as well. The farm was sold and my sister and her family had to relocate.

In the end, the estate dispute was settled out of court with them offering the two of us a small cut.

A few years later, my younger sister and Mom had a huge fight, which resulted in years of not speaking.

I didn't really know what it was about. Everyone kept quite as usual. Later, it came out that the rift happened because Mom changed her story telling her Mac was not actually her father, that she was in fact Dad's child.

Mom told her she knew I "Baby" as Mac called me was to weak-willed to go to the lawyer and that she got paid well for playing her part in the charade, by getting a cut of the estate.

Now that brought up a lot more questions. How did Mom get all of these friends to write letters to the lawyer stating these lies?

How did she do it and why did she do it? These people she coaxed to do this on her behalf were all good upstanding citizens.

We all wonder how she got these two men, Dad and Mac, to go along with her shenanigans all her life.

In essence, how did she get a community of people to play these roles she created for them? Why did I go along? Think of the damage it did to my sister.

After a lot of insight and learning to work with my intuition, I had a vision that I believe is true. What if... there was indeed a will?

I believe Mac gave it to Mom for safe keeping. I know he was told to get his affairs in order.

I had a feeling

I felt she had the will, knowing I was the beneficiary, which never worried her or upset her because she had a plan of her own. No one would ever see the will anyway.

Upon Mac's death she would destroy the will. She would have the farm, assets and his money. She was his partner, finally she would have what she believed she deserved.

Things were moving fast that morning, and the shock of his death sent her spiraling out of control. She had to act fast because Mac's brother was on his way to take care of the estate.

In a panic, she had to take care of that will fast. Quickly completing that task would put her in control, where she could call the shots.

My sister and her family could stay on the farm. She would give me some part of the estate, she would make things good for us girls, as she always stated was her intention when things happened.

She felt strongly she was Mac's partner. It was plain to see they were a couple. I believe she thought she had it in the bag, if he didn't have a will, she would be entitled to the whole estate as any wife or partner would be.

However her plan backfired. She didn't take into consideration she was in fact married and living in the same house with her husband as well.

Meditating upon the issue, it came to me that the will was destroyed by my Mother.

I saw her sitting at the kitchen table with a homemade will written on a yellowed nine by thirteen paper. I could see her flicking her lighter, holding the flame at the bottom corner of the paper, it going up in smoke, curling up as pieces of the paper burned and fell. Until she was left with nothing but little pieces of blacken paper on the table. I could see her hurrying to clean it up.

I believe when she realized it would not go to her, she was beside herself. How could she fix this awful mistake? Because I would not play into the role she created for me to cover up her mistake, she had to get my sister involved.

The people in the community, along with everyone that knew Mac, knew he did not want that farm going to his siblings.

He had built the farm to what it was with his bare hands. His blood, sweat and tears. His life energy went into it, to make it what it was at his passing.

How she got the six people to do what they did is hard for me to understand. I can hear her confessing to each of them that she had done an awful thing and could they help her put things straight?

I believe they did it because of Mac, knowing it is what he would have wanted. They could only go off of what he had told them in his lifetime and what story she provided them with.

Repeating the Past

When Mom passed, she had also left a hand written will. She had told me about it and shown it to me.

She explained to me how she had enough money in her bank account to give each of us kids some money. She also stated that she wanted us to have that money and it was not to go to Dad.

Upon her death, Dad asked us girls to clear out Mom's personal things and divide up what we wanted. During this process, her handwritten will showed up.

We stood in a circle, around a pile of garbage, in the middle of the kitchen floor. My oldest sister read it out loud. We realized that we had already done everything the way she wanted it to be done as far as personal belongings.

The will did indeed state that her money should be divided between her seven kids. If she had not left a will, the money would have gone to Dad. The money going to us kids now would be fine but what happens in the future.

We discussed whether or not to take the money now, doing what Mom stated in her will.

We could see that it would pose another problem. What if Dad ran out of money or needed medical care or a nursing home, it would be very expensive.

Should we take the money now like she stated and pay it back to Dad in the event he needs it?

We all knew it is a lot easier to leave the money to Dad now than pay back later. He already had funeral expenses, which would deplete his account substantially. With Mom gone the disposable income was also gone.

We all agreed the money would go to Dad to pay her funeral expenses. The will was tossed into that pile of garbage in the middle of the kitchen floor.

How ironic that we nonchalantly tossed her will. Never did it cross our minds that we were destroying her will nor did it cross my mind until long after Mac's death that she destroyed his. What goes around comes around.

We did get the money when Dad passed, so eventually her wishes were carried out, just not at the time she wanted them to be.

Dads will in turn, was written in a law office. Executors were named and things were legal. My older brother was executor and I was co-executor.

After the wills were signed and ready to go, the lawyer handed the will to my brother. Dad told my brother to give the will to me, that I would be taking care of it.

Even when the Lawyer tried explaining to him, the Executor holds the will. He said "No, I want her to have the will." He was adamant that I keep it in my possession, saying I was his book keeper and that I took care of him. I did take care of his details.

When I saw my vision of Mom burning Mac's will, it came

to me why Dad was so adamant, the reason why Dad did not want anyone else to have his will.

First, because of my lot in this family he wanted to make sure I was given my one-seventh share. It was possible he had already seen Mac's will destroyed.

He was unaware if you have a legal will there is more than one copy.

I found out first hand settling an estate is a lot of work. My husband and I used our money when Dad's estate was in probate. We paid for all the household expenses and materials to get the house ready for sale.

I cleaned his house for years, not accepting any payment he offered. I felt it was the least I could do for all he had done for me in my life.

My husband and boys did the gutting of the basement to get it ready for sale. It took two and a half years to settle the estate.

Dealing with Dads estate, opened up more thoughts about Mac. Thinking back on Mac's death it came to me that some of the people that wrote the letters claiming my sister and I were his daughters are still living.

I know I could, ask some questions, hear yet another story about the past and why they offered to help Mom. Going into it deeper I realize I have heard enough. Why put myself through more torment?

I don't believe I need to talk to anyone. I lived with these people in this toxic environment. I know more than a neighbor would know.

I have never been told the straight forward truth by anyone in my life regarding this topic, why would it be different now? I am depending solely on myself. My intuition is strong and I trust myself.

Being so close to Mac while he was alive and the confirmation from Mom stating he was he my farther, did mix my emotions and brought up a lot of unanswered questions.

Where would I get the answers? Who could I trust, anyway? It was a huge secret. How could I even ask anyone anything? I wasn't even sure if Dad knew anything about this when I was younger.

I understand now that I had been the only one keeping the secret. Apparently everyone else always knew. I also realized that Mac and Mom went everywhere together, because Dad always worked, and she wanted to get out.

I could have asked Mac's friends some of my questions, but really, if I could not trust him or Mom, how could I expect to get any truth from them?

None of my older sibling shed light on anything and I didn't ask. If I asked Mom she would always tell me to let it go. Nothing will bring him back. Some things are best left alone. And so I did.

I had a lot to be grateful for. I had a great husband and two amazing little boys. I focused all of my energy on my own family. Days were filled with after school activities and many hockey games. Eleven years after my second son was born, we were blessed with our amazing daughter. It was fun having a little girl in the house. We were able to create lots of happy memories as a family.

My husband and I owned a couple of businesses. He worked nonstop and I took care of the children and all the business clerical details. I also worked in a school setting as a teacher's assistant while our daughter attended grades two through eight.

Nevertheless, I continued to be anxious and never understood how deeply my tumultuous childhood had affected me.

Mom and Dad returned to what appeared to be more of a normal married life after Mac passed away in 1984.

Mom passed in 1998 at the age of seventy-eight. Dad lived until the great age of ninety-six, leaving this earth in 2007. He believed his longevity was attributed to working hard six days a week. Sundays were to relax and go fishing.

He was well known for all the miles he walked as a young man. He went hunting providing meat for his family. He loved to read and watch sports. In his later years he loved to played crib at the Legion with his friends.

He lived in his own home and drove until his ninety sixth birthday. He kept to his schedule no matter what.

CHAPTER FIVE

Strong Intuition

I have strong intuition. Over the years, I have been using it more and more recognizing that all the answers are in me.

EFT and meditation have opened me up to the possibility of allowing myself to finally take a look at my past.

I have had some wonderful revelations, as well as a lot more questions coming to the surface.

Over the last few years, I find that more aliments and diseases are showing up in my body.

I am noticing my patterns. I am becoming aware of how many times I have brought people into my life that treat me the way Mom treated me.

How many times I have been kept in the dark about things,

how many times I have chose to stay in the dark. I have been lied to, and robbed of my rights. I gave my power away.

I now recognize when I am being manipulated. I have learned to say no when I mean no. Though I struggled with that, always believing I was a bad person or selfish if I said no, I now say no more often than yes to others. Yes more often to myself.

I allow things to come to me. I have come a long way in the past few years using EFT. I have learned to set boundaries.

Boundaries

I first learned about boundaries when I began working at my daughter's school as a teacher's assistant. One of the counsellors talked about setting boundaries. I found the concept to be totally out of my realm of thinking at the time. I wondered if I even had any.

She explained that they are kind of like your limits. Oh, I knew I had limits. When I reached my limit, I blew up, so I knew I had limits. She said limits are how you establish your boundaries.

Now I understand how boundaries work. They are set by me, for me, a place that works for me. It has nothing to do with pushing myself to the limit.

She also said learning to say no would be one of the things I would benefit from. She suggested that I read a book on the topic. I didn't think that would work for me. How could I tell people no? I couldn't say no to anyone but my husband, who always joked that I had no problem saying no to him. I realized I said no to myself all the time.

Yet, when faced by others requests, I felt powerless, hot, anxious, and guilty at the thought of saying no. I didn't want to let anyone down. I wanted to be good person.

Then Mom's voice would pop up in my head. "I thought for sure you would do this for me. I thought I could count on you. You won't let Mom down, will you? I know the others won't help dear old Mom, but I know you will."

I always bought in to her guilt and manipulation. She played me like a fiddle until the day she died. She always said, "I love you, honey, even though you wrecked my life." I loved her too, no matter what.

I felt indebted to Mom, Dad, and Mac, as well as my sibling at times. EFT help me go deeper into these areas of my life, I can see how I allowed people to play me, how I bought it in and why. I wanted to be loved and accepted. I wanted to make up for the fact that I was born and wrecked their lives. I bent over backwards trying to set it all straight.

I was guilty taking the money from Dad's estate.

Boundaries.... How would I have known anything about boundaries, let alone know how to set them?

I brought all of my family's turmoil with me everywhere I went and created more of my own. I was exceptional at burying things deep inside so I wouldn't feel the pain.

In my adult life, as I raised my kids, the door of my home was open to whatever or whoever wanted in. I went with the flow; or more like went with the whirl wind and cooked for everyone that stopped by.

I provided support for everyone in my life, whether it was listening to their problems or providing a place for them to stay. I would find myself babysitting or cleaning their houses. I reach my limit many times.

My intentions were to be helpful and try to make their day better, like I did for Mom. Did it work for me? No! I found I was exhausted and behind in my own work. While they sat with their feet up I was working late into the night to stay on top of things.

I chose to do this, I can only blame myself. It filled a need of some kind. A need to be praised, or maybe it became a habit in my child hood, I did honestly believe I was helping.

When I reached that point, Mom would tell others I was having a nervous breakdown because I would blow up. She would tell me to fight those feelings. To fight, fight, fight, and then she would tell me how much worse her life was in comparison.

I was absolutely the best at fighting myself. I could build a case against myself beyond my worst nightmares.

So I would do just that—I would push down more of myself, more anger, more hurt, more suffering, I would read another self-help book, learn a new coping strategy.

I would feel guilty because everyone thought I was having a nervous breakdown, which fed into their belief that I was weak. I felt like a blown up punching bag. The harder someone would punch me down, the quicker I would rebound.

I prided myself on a quick recovery because I had too much to do to stay down too long. So I endured and suffered, never thinking about what I needed, or how to fit myself in.

That is exactly what it was. I NEVER FIT ANYWHERE. From the time of my conception until the day I was introduced to EFT, I did not realize how deeply this pain and emotional stress affected me. It went to my core.

I was not self-aware, nor did I understand its devastating effect on my health...until I started digging, uncovering my past. EFT showed me that I have the right to find the root of my issue. I have the right to understand how it affected me and how I played in to it. I finally learned about boundaries and how to set them.

Learning that it is my right, I took my power back. I began making the decisions for my own life. It wasn't an overnight process; I took it one step at a time. I read, tapped, learned to meditate, silenced the critical voices and listened to my gut.

Slowly, I went from a place of being used and abused, lied to, cheated out of experiences and stolen from, to a place where I decide what I will do, for who and when I will do it.

I have moved from the bottom rung of the ladder to sitting on the top rung, looking out at what I have access to and what I will choose for myself and my family.

One last note, where would I have learned about boundaries? OBVOIUSLY NOT FROM MY FAMILY.

I believe my anxiety and the toxic energy around me

started in the womb. Can you imagine? I can feel all the pain and suffering my Mom went through.

I was carrying the burden of her pain before I was even born, let alone all the pain my Dad and older siblings felt.

I could also feel the confusion my biological father Mac felt, at the age of twenty-two, wondering what in the world he was going to do. I was his child. Where did he fit in?

Who Had Control?

I realize there is nothing I can do to change the past. My parents did the best that they knew how to do. They made their choices for reasons of their own, and I use to believe it was to protect me. Now I believe it had nothing to do with me, they were protecting themselves.

My guilt over wrecking the family when I was born, turned into guilt over what I did when I was eight, running into the living room to ask Dad if Mac could live with us.

Up to that point the family was intact: Dad, Mom and us seven children. We could pretend we were "normal." in our eyes and the eyes of the community. I have said many times, it was hard on my older siblings; they knew the whole story and lived through a different set of circumstance.

My brother started drinking around the time Mac moved it, spending a lot of time at our oldest sisters. He would have friends over, and they would have drinks before a dance or going out. Mom was not happy about that.

The energy in the house was so toxic at times. I carried a lot of guilt, even for being born. I felt that I shamed the family. I took on all of Mom's guilt and pain.

I realize now where the shame actually lied, and who made the choices that led to this outcome. I was the result of their choices.

CHAPTER
SIX

Imagine
How did we get here?

Even though most of us do not believe we get to choose our parents, there are some individuals that have written books asserting that we do choose them. Thinking in that context, I was wondering what and how that would work.

Just for fun, I imagined if this was my case. Interestingly enough, we can look at any perspective we want at any time. We have incredible minds.

Sometime it is okay to look outside the box. You may find something interesting. I love being open to all kinds of ideas. It has helped me become more aware of the world around me.

I can see myself sitting where ever baby souls come from,

listening to the attributes this child would need to be placed in this family here on earth.

She must be accepting and honorable and sure of herself, so sure that she believes she can do anything. Knowing she can do it, she will find herself facing many issues in her life. Even though she knows this before she accepts this family, she will forget it all upon her birth.

All the answers to all of her questions lay deep in her soul. All she has to do is ask, but, she will only be given what she can handle at the time.

Lessons will be learned along the way. Wisdom will start to show up in many places, intuition will take root. She will start to trust herself more and more.

When she gets to the place of allowing good to come to her, her world will open up like never before.

The Assignment

Baby girl will be born late March 1956. She will need to be accepting of others. She will place number six in this large family.

There will be turmoil and upset along the way, she must learn to adapt to difficult situations. She needs to be able to persevere under pressure.

She will encounter a lot of colds, ear aches, and tonsillitis, stomach disorders and anxiety as a child, carrying these ailments with her all of her life.

She will grow up believing she is being raised in a normal, healthy home. She will have a younger sister when she is two years old, completing the family unit.

She will be provided for and will be the first child to graduate from grade twelve. She will have the opportunity to learn a lot in her lifetime, all of which will lead her to write a book in her sixtieth year of life.

She will grow up watching her life unfold in a normal, everyday fashion. It won't be until she is older that she will understand the dysfunctional state of her family.

She won't believe what people will say, and will always honor her mother and father no matter what.

As she get older she will find out she has been lied to, kept in the dark about all the family secrets. That nothing in her life is what she thought it was. Even her birth certificate is a lie.

She will be the result of an extramarital affair. Her mother will remain living in the family home with her husband.

After years of a neighboring man spending every day at your home he will move in as a boarder, and he and her mother will spend even more time together as a couple, this child will be ignorant of everything that is happening around her.

Then one day she will learn that the boarder is her biological father. She will play along with all the lies and deception, thinking that is the way things are until one day she will come to a place in her life where she is ready to know the truth.

She will be introduced to a new way of thinking, a technique that will change her life.

It will be like an awakening, a new beginning. She will start thinking outside the box. She will let the toxic feelings out, understanding more and more. The time is NOW to finally put the lying and deception to rest.

Understanding the Facts

My birth certificate is a lie. It states that Mom's husband is my father.

He raised and provided for me until I was seventeen, when I moved out on my own. He was my Dad in my eyes until the day of his passing. He raised me as his own.

Everyone in the community knew I was the illegitimate child. My biological grandparents knew. My biological father knew as well, hence his involvement in my life.

My older sibling knew. There was this incredible secret that they all lived with, keeping me in the dark.

I was raised in a dysfunctional home.

I could feel the pain yet never understood what it was or its source.

I accepted my mother's husband as my Dad; yet, I felt the boarder was more like a father in a lot of ways. If I needed something, he was there.

Understanding the Truth of my Family Dynamics

My true family was Mac, Mom and Me. I was an only child in that unit.

We lived with my Mother, her husband and their six children. I have six step-siblings.

I knew Mac's family well and visited them. I spent time with his parents. His dad passed when I was very young, but I have fond memories of him.

I called Mac's mother Grandma because we called older ladies my parents knew Grandma. She spent time at our house, a great lady. I always gave my room to her when she visited. I was told I had no grandparents.

At the passing of my biological father, there was no Last Will and Testament found and no legal beneficiary. The law stated that his estate would go to the nearest living relative. He had no wife, and only one child (me), which would have made me the beneficiary of his estate. However, that was not the case because my birth certificate stated otherwise.

Accepting and Living with the Lies

I was born into this family; how I got here was unique, to say the least. Even though it was dysfunctional by societal standards, it was my life. I accepted everyone involved because I would not be here otherwise. Blind acceptance became my coping mechanism.

I never realized I was repeating the same pattern by accepting these lies as truth for me and my children.

Not only was I being lied to, I was accepting these lies and passing them on to my children, and after the birth of my granddaughter, I would be still passing it to the next generation.

This is where the lies must stop. The family tree will state who my biological father and my biological parents are.

As for my acting and providing father, my dear Dad, his memories will also be honored into the generations as a huge part of my life. By honouring myself, I will be able to honor each one of them.

Accepting my True Identity

I am Mac's daughter. I accept him as my legal father, even if the birth certificate states otherwise.

The man I called Dad was my stepfather. I am ever so grateful for all that he did for me. His acceptance of me and the relationship we shared is second to none. I have let go of all my fear of dishonoring him by accepting my biological father.

I feel like I am honoring myself and the people in my life in a healthy way and from a true perspective.

I thank Dad for the relationship he had with my children and my husband. He was a wonderful man who spent his entire life providing for his family.

Tommy's Last Will and Testament

At the grand age of ninety-five and after a hospital stay, Dad finally decided to write his will. He agreed to talk to a lawyer when I informed him that laws had changed and his estate would not automatically go to his seven children as he believed.

His youngest son had lived with him for years and he would be granted the estate. He was appalled by the law, and did not hesitate to go to the lawyer and put his affairs in order.

He decided that his eldest son would be executor and I would be co-executor. Together, we took him to the lawyer. He still lived in his own home and would remain there until his passing,

In a previous conversation with the lawyer, I had mentioned the history of my family. We discussed in private the details of Dad's biological children.

Dad also spoke to him in private as well discussing the issue of biological children. In the end, his will read: "I have seven children, biological or not, who I raised as my own. My wish is to divide my estate equally between my seven children. It is what I want and what their mother wanted."

And so it was.

CHAPTER SEVEN

Why Did They All Stay Together?

People often ask me why my Dad stayed in a situation like that. Why didn't he leave or kick Mom or Mac out?

His story does shed some light and a little understanding as to why he made the choices he did.

When Dad was just seven years old, his mother died giving birth to his sister, leaving his father alone with two boys and a newborn.

It was decided that his father would leave Scotland and come to Canada, where his sister would help him raise the two boys. He planned to bring his daughter when he was settled.

After a year and a half, his father decided he did not like living in Canada. He packed up his few belonging and returned to Scotland.

Both boys were left in the care of their Aunt, who they had just met the year before.

Imagine being eight years old, and having lost both your mother and your father. I believe that he vowed to himself if he ever had a family, he would never abandon them, no matter what.

Why Didn't Mom Leave?

She had seven kids to provide for and a roof over her head to maintain. It was not her choice to marry Dad. After becoming pregnant, her father insisted that she marry him.

He felt Dad would be a good provider and husband. She lost control of any future choice to marry the man she says she loved.

Her life was created by her own doing as all of our lives are. Her choices were not in her best interest most of the time.

Image the shame and guilt she felt as she carried on with the neighbor behind Dad's back. Image the ridicule, the hate she felt for herself.

Her goal in life was to be loved, but she looked for love in all the wrong places. She didn't get to make the choice she should have been free to make.

What if she could have had some control over her life? What if someone could have given her the love she needed? More importantly, WHAT IF SHE COULD HAVE LOVED HERSELF?

I know she sacrificed a lot. She spent more than forty years of her life caring for her children living under her roof.

Apart from the affairs she never ever fulfilled her own needs. She spent many nights at home with all us kids while Dad and Mac would be doing their own things.

She went on to have twenty-two grandchildren. Her first grandchild was born nine months after her last child.

I could not imagine doing what she did in the era she did it. I came to believe she did the best she knew how to do. At least that is what she told me all the time.

Why Didn't Mac Just Move On?

It would have made sense for him to walk away. He was only twenty-two years old and trapped in a tangled web with a thirty-six-year-old married woman with five children and a husband.

He could have easily turned his back on the whole situation. No one would have been the wiser. Both his family and our family would have remained intact and all would have been well, in society's eyes at least.

But he didn't choose the easy way out. He claimed what was his and chose to love and be part of his daughter life. He decided to be a hands-on father, no matter what anyone thought. How can I hold that against him? The fact that he kept it a secret is not cool.

Even though I don't understand why everything panned

out as it did, I know they tried to have my best interest at heart.

She was my mother and I accept her as she was, now and forever. There were three of them; any one of them could have chosen to tell me the truth at any time but they didn't. That was their choice.

Even though I have been asked how I dealt with all that, I respond by saying that if it were not for their choices, I would not be here. I had three parents, all of whom loved me in their own way. I may have been a frail, weak, sickly kid as Mom would say, but that was then and this is now.

I am now a strong, caring, forgiving adult who loves to learn. I did my very best at raising my children, but I made my own mistakes along the way.

None of us know what or how much we don't know. What secrets are buried in your family? My bet is that there is a lot more that is unknown to all of us than we believe.

I am grateful and thankful that I had these three extraordinary individuals as my parents. My perspective has changed. I have opened up to the possibility of seeing, feeling, and living life from a new perspective.

Why Didn't I Ask More Questions?

As I look back at the past, I sometimes wonder why I didn't ask more questions. I wonder why I didn't poke and prod more and demand answers.

I could have accepted Mac as my father at age sixteen when I first came into this knowledge. Or I could have accepted him at twenty-eight when he passed away and Mom admitted it all to me.

I see now that I was not ready. I chose to push it down and live what I thought would be a normal life. Then I realized I was hurting myself by denying this part of my story; I felt frustrated and emotionally crippled.

I didn't realize how much it affected me until I opened up to knowing. I was living a lie and I made that choice. I now choose to live my truth.

CHAPTER EIGHT

Our Little Miracle

My first grandchild was born on my Mom's birthday. I will admit I had a couple of "Oh no! Not today!" moments.

I worried some of this bad energy I felt would be passed down to my sweet little grandchild.

As my daughter-in-law's labor progressed and complications arose, I found myself wishing that all three of my parents were there. Coming closer to the delivery time, I realized that they were there in spirit, giving us all strength.

As I looked at my beautiful grandbaby, I was elated. I was so happy, so proud, and so exhausted from the worry for both my daughter in-law and my grandchild.

I left the hospital an emotional wreck. My daughter in-law had a very long labor. I stayed with them during the entire labor, leaving just before the delivery, with the rest of our family spending hours in the waiting room, checking in to be part of this amazing time. Also running for anything we needed from pillows to hot coffee.

My son called me later that night. He knew I was overjoyed and very emotional. I mentioned the date.

His response blew me away. He told me, "My daughter, your granddaughter, was born on exactly the right day. The perfect day, it is a new beginning of happy times to come."

He told me that it was time to lay the issues with my mother to rest. His wife's Grandmother, (mama) was praying their baby would be born June second to change the energy of the day her own son died.

He said, "The universe thought you needed it more. Mama has dealt with her pain, but you never dealt with yours. The time is now.

You need to understand something. There was a high chance that my daughter may not be with us right now.

The umbilical cord was tied in a knot and there were two placentas. The doctor informed us that there was a forty-five percent mortality rate."

With those words, the flood gates opened and my healing began. I whispered, "Thank you, Mom."

During the birth my daughter in-law had something of her Papa's that she was given when he passed; she held it close to her heart the whole time.

I could also feel Mac's presence and then my Mom's. I felt her excitement.

Breathing deep and looking at a picture of daisies on the hospital wall, I could sense my mother-in-law was there in spirit as well. She loved daisies.

Power of the Spirit and the Miracle of Life

Everyone we needed was there to welcome our dear grand-daughter, into this world.

Getting to know my little granddaughter over the past six months has been the most uplifting and personally fulfilling experience at this stage of my life.

She is a sweet soul; her smiles light up a room. She is the calm in the eye of a storm. She has brought purpose and blessing to her parents, creating a healthy and happy atmosphere.

Her being born on my Mom's birthday has healed a lot of pain in my heart, replacing sorrowful memories with joyful ones.

I have come to accept Mom on a much deeper level. I feel her memory as uplifting now.

Being a grandmother has brought me to a new place of self-understanding. I find myself saying "sorry, Mom" on so many levels. I find myself acting like her, asking my son and his wife for the same things Mom asked me for. Seeing clearer the things I never understood.

The birth, the presence of the spirits of Mom and Mac at

the delivery has given me so much more love for what I have in my life.

I do see more clearly, I love more deeply and I am grateful for the miracles that have been sent our way.

I see tremendous growth in my son and his wife, reacting to their beautiful miracle.

I watch in awe as my daughter evolves into a hands-on aunty, building a strong connection with her sister-in-law. My son the baby's uncle, showers his niece with love.

With her giggles, her infectious smile, her innocence and her untainted love, she has brought healing to us all.

CHAPTER NINE

How to Tap Into the Root of Issues

There are many forms of self-healing. EFT is a healing process that sees the importance of clearing the root of a problem or issue. If the root of the issue is not found, you will keep experiencing all of the same emotions. The root is the key that needs to be released.

It is like having a bowl of crap and trying to cover it up with strawberries and whipped cream. You still have the crap.

It takes some time to get to the root in conventional ways. With EFT, it can happen within minutes. An understanding of what it is and where you are holding it in your body comes to the surface.

The root is what stops us from moving forward. It is the source of all the blocks. If you can identify it, you will find success quickly. There may be a lot of roots each emotion could have a root of its own, attacking more than one part of your body.

The Book You Can Heal Your Life by Louise Hay outlines what illness is created by which emotion. That will give you a starting point to begin your EFT journey. You will also find it on line.

EFT is a simple technique with only a few steps. Tapping smooth's out our body's energy system, opening us up to the possibility of understanding what is really going on.

It gives us relief, enough to think clearly, to go into our subconscious and to see what is stored there. You may be amazed at what you find. All of the answers to anything you need to know are within you.

I read somewhere that human beings only use about ten percent of our brains. Maybe the other ninety percent is storing the crap I talked about earlier.

LET IT GO.

How often have you heard someone say "Let it go?" What does that mean, anyway?

We can be in the middle of the same haunting problem that is tormenting us, and someone says, "Let it go."

When I heard that, I would automatically think, "How can I let this go?" I would then feel foolish for even mentioning it out loud again, yet the feeling would persist and cause me even more pain. It would come out as a headache, stomach upset or something much worse.

I do not listen to anyone telling me that now. I have every right to have that feeling. I will keep having that feeling come up until I finally make the decision to stop and find out what the root of the torment is.

The people that tell you to let it go are not trying to be mean. They just don't want to hear about it anymore. When I get that feeling now, I know there is a message of some kind.

Always start tapping on the Karate Chop point when you start asking yourself these questions: I make time to look at the feeling, where is it coming from? What do I think is causing it?

It will probably come from something someone said to trigger it, or perhaps because you did something you feel guilty about.

It may not be what you think it is. What has just happened to upset you? Is it the thing that brought you to this same point before in your life?

It will usually have something to do with your past, far back in your childhood. Go back as far as you can remember and ask yourself when you first felt this. Look at that situation. How did that make you feel then?

As soon as you recognize that time in your life, the energy will start to shift. You may feel angrier or more hurt at this point.

That is perfectly fine and an indication that you are moving in the right direction. You have touched on the root. If you start to cry, let yourself cry.

If you feel a pain in your body somewhere, or a stabbing sensation in your heart, or shortness of breath, honor these feelings. It is important that you allow yourself the freedom to open up to the possibility of a revelation. Or you can stop and try again later. Always be kind to yourself.

Tap on the things that came up while repeating the set up statement. Go through all the tapping points starting on the top of your head.

Example: Even though I feel this coming up, I do not know what it is. I accept that I do not yet know what it is. I accept what is coming up.

Accept the feeling, even though it may not be easy. You have the right to feel what you feel. Accept yourself even if it is hard right now.

Find the part of the body that is being affected. It could be the head, in your neck, between your shoulders, top middle or lower back, heart, stomach, chest, joints, etc. Give it a number between one and ten. Zero, being perfectly fine, ten being the worst.

Give it a colour. What does that colour mean to you? Red means anger, black means grief for some. Use what you believe to be true for you.

Give it an emotion. Is it anger, fear, guilt, resentment, or grief? Name the emotion. If there are two, go with the one that is really showing its true colours first.

Give it a texture. Is it sharp, pointed, rough, bumpy, or smooth?

Give it a size. Is it heavy, huge, long, the size of a house, the world, or a basketball?

It may sound something like this....

Even though I am extremely upset right now, I accept myself. (Repeat three times) Even though I am extremely upset, I feel like my head is going to explode, I can't take it anymore. I have had enough, I want this to stop.

I am so angry at what is happing and it always happens to me. I accept that I do see it is always happening to me. Wow, it is always happening to me. I do not want to feel this way. Right now, I have no control over any of this. It is a number ten for sure. I feel like my head is going to explode.

I accept that I feel this right now. I have no control over this issue. I accept that. It feels like a volcano is going to erupt in my head. It is red-hot, and looks like lava.

I accept myself no matter what is going on in my head right now. Even though I have this horrible hot lava trying to erupt in my head and causing me all this pain, I can tap.

I can see what is happening to me right now. It feels very scary. My issue is very scary. I am angry and I am scared. (Repeat three time moving between tapping points starting on the top of your head and moving through each point.)

Even though I feel angry and scared, I am willing to help

myself. I can see this is not a good place to be. I have a volcano ready to erupt in my head.

Who put it there? I don't think I put it there. It was this issue and that person that did this to me. This always happens to me. (Repeat three times)

Think back to the first time you ever felt like your head was going to explode. What age were you? What happened?

Even though I was very young the first time this happened, I felt so angry. I remember that day. How could that have anything to do with today? Could there be a connection?

Repeat three times: Even though I was very young, I had the exact same feeling as I do now. I had the exact same feeling. Wow! It has been happening to me for many years.

What if? What if this is the cause of my pent-up anger? What if I am carrying all of this and adding to it every time a situation comes to the surface? What if I could take a look at this issue today, from my adult age?

Would that change anything in me? I think it will make a difference if I take a look at that day.

If I am the one holding all of this anger, which I guess I am, no one else can get in my body to do this to me. Maybe I do have some control. I do have some control. I do have control over this. Even though I am not sure what to do to get rid of this feeling in my head, I want it gone.

At this point, your energy will be shifting. The number should be dropping, maybe to an eight.

I am willing to try and let go. Even a little will take off the pressure. I choose to release some of this pressure I feel in my head, the number may drop to a seven.

I choose to let go of the pain from that day so very long ago. I accept that I have more control that I believed. I have control of me. The number may drop to a four.

My body doesn't like anger. I am tired of being scared. What if I could let go of the rest of this explosive feeling in my head? I am ready let go of the heat in my head. I can release the pressure, the heat is gone. The volcano no longer looks like a volcano. It may be more the size of a marble. It is hard now and has a message.

Ask yourself what the message is. Ask the question you wish you could have asked the first time you felt this feeling many years ago.

Silence your head and go to your gut for the answer. What do you want to do with this information? What do you want to do with the marble?

Repeat three times: I am in control of me. I choose what I let in my body.

Close your eyes, relax, let the energy flow through your body, starting from the top of your head.

Visualize the energy moving out any remaining negative thoughts from your brain, relax your jaw, your shoulder, your spinal cord, each organ, limbs, blood vessels, each and every cell in your body. Let it go. Feel the energy flowing.

Pat yourself on the back. Imagine this feeling. Imagine feeling this light every day.

You are the one that created the issue you felt, you are the one that took the time to understand it, and you made the final decision as to what to do with it.

Who has the power? YOU DO!

CHAPTER
TEN

How to Release the Root

I spent a lot of time contemplating what I would say to end the book. Never in my wildest imagination did I think this is what would come to be, my morning tapping and meditation session.

Every fall we spend time somewhere warm. This year I decided to use some of my time here to work on my book.

I went out to the lovely pool area and sat under the shade of the bountiful palms of the palm tree, breathing in the wonderful scent of the flowers. It was overcast, with a breeze, and the blue water in the pool rippled gently.

It was a perfect place to tap and meditate. I had been feeling many different emotions leading up to this day.

I had just finished writing my personal perspective, about

the wills and all the lies. My heart was heavy. Each time I write, it stirs my emotions.

I felt guilt, anger, humiliation and fear of going forward with this book. I began tapping on these feelings.

I felt guilty writing this story, like I was betraying my family. The realization that I was always thinking of others first came up right away. Tapping on that, a thought crossed my mind: what about the betrayal I had to overcome?

I was angry because not only had all three parents of mine hidden the truth from me, so had my siblings, who ranged from eight to eighteen years older than me.

Our entire community knew this secret about me. I felt like I was the center of a conspiracy, the odd specimen under the scrutiny of a magnifying lens. It was a humiliating sensation.

I was also riddled with doubt as to whether I should even continue with this story and publish my book.

I felt hurt and deflated to think I was a small child living in the dark, while everyone shone their negative light on me, making me feel like I was not one of them. I had been deeply, irrevocably betrayed. I know that none of this was my fault. They created this mess, not me.

I knew I had to let go of these feelings so I could see things from a true perspective. I had to move forward without this burden on my shoulders, and in my stomach.

I replayed the memory in my head, allowing these feeling to surface. In my mind's eye, I examined each thought and feeling. I saw a small child placed in a situation where everyone walked around her on egg shells.

They knew a secret but didn't dare to tell her. They feared Mom and Mac, and maybe Dad as well.

Dad was a good man. He owned the country store and never wanted us to say bad things about anyone. We were the center of the little hamlet we lived in.

I could see more people than I ever realized knew my story because when I started to open up about the truth, my husband's sisters-in-law knew as well.

I would hear words like, "We always knew. It was common knowledge. You are the only one that didn't know."

During my teen years after first hearing of this, I never got any answers, so I just grew immune to the taunting. I decided to believe what I had always believed, that Dad was my real father.

Tapping, sifting and sorting through these thoughts, it came to me that I am not alone. A lot of people are in similar situations. If not with the other man living in their house, certainly with the pain and suffering of their own personal story.

I decided I would go to my intuition. I would write the last chapter as it was revealed to me during this early morning tapping and meditation. See what comes up…. release it and move forward.

If I can help one person find their way to this unbelievable tool called EFT (tapping), if one person can learn to stop the chatter in their head, go to their intuition; trust their own gut, if they could understand that all answers are within them. Then it would be worth all my effort and I would be healed in the process. Win-Win.

My story needs to be told.

I have not only found my way to inner peace, I am going beyond my wildest dreams, writing this book, sharing steps of my healing journey.

How it Unfolded

Even though I am feeling overwhelmed, and unsure, I want to finish my book. Even though I am just hitting a wall of fear that I am not good enough, or smart enough, I accept these feelings.

Even though I am extremely angry at all the people in my life that lied and betrayed me over the years, I do want to write my book, and most of all, publish my book.

I know this is a stretch for me, yet the writing and tapping have been easy for me. I am at the end, at the final chapter. I am grateful for that.

I want to do whatever it is I have to do to get to the end of this journey with my family issues.

I want to let it go, to set myself free. I want to know why I carried this heavy burden all my life......attracting more of the same kind of people into my life treating me exactly the same way I was treated as a child..

I want to know why I have an autoimmune disorder, where my body attacks itself.

I was told I have an overactive immune system. Why is it overactive? Where in my life have I been overactive? I know I can get hyper, overanxious, overwhelmed. My mind races, I have held a lot of pain, anger and fear in my body. I accept myself anyway.

Even though I have done all of these things creating a lot of disease in my body, I accept myself anyway. I have diabetes. I accept that I played a huge role in all of these issues in my body.

I accept some of it came from my childhood, starting at conception. I accept I didn't know how to deal with all of these issues. I understand myself better now, and I love and accept that.

I can see we all did the best we knew how to do at the time. I could have dropped all these unfixable issues when I first heard of them, had I known then what I know now.

I could have held my head high, knowing we all have been affected by this issue. I am not alone. I deeply and completely accept where I have come from and how far I have come on this EFT healing journey.

I thank the universe for all I have been able to achieve. I thank myself for persevering through each and every emotional trauma.

I am ever so grateful I was able to open myself up to my intuition. I realize I am the one doing this to myself. I can help myself. No one can fix anyone else. We only have the power to heal ourselves.

It is up to me to be open to the possibilities of moving forward, creating new thought patterns and outcomes. I accept and honor myself once and for all. It is my time. I can change my perspective. I cannot change the past, but I can look at it from a different perspective, seeing myself not as the victim but as the survivor.

Another thought surfaces, nothing can live without food.

What if I stop feeding the victim in me, what have I been feeding it anyway? Thinking, I come to see, I have been feeding it negative thoughts almost every day.

It seems to be a need in me. I am feeding the need to feel this way. I am stuck at that place in my life where I saw myself as a victim. I put myself in that box and labeled it Victim.

Wow! That is not what I want now, I told myself to get out of that box. Why are you sitting in that box? Look at all the negative things you put in that box. I had a look at what I was feeding myself. I saw piles of negative thoughts.

I knew I had a choice, I could stay in the box and fight with myself or I could decide I wanted better.

What is better? Being a survivor came to mind. I jumped out of that box so fast, threw all of the negative thoughts and emotional pain in the box. I closed the lid and walked away, I am done with being a victim.

I am a survivor, I could feel a shift in my energy, I felt elated and energized, I knew I had let go of all the blocked energy.

I chose to claim a new perspective. I can make new chooses, I can do what I would like to do. I will be open to feeding the survivor in me, positive uplifting healthy thoughts. I will show love and kindness to the survivor in me.

What if none of this would have been in my life? I would not be telling my story today. What if it was a lot worse?

Light bulb moment.....

What if it was a lot worse? I am so grateful I was lucky enough to be in a family that overcame all the obstacles, no matter how dysfunctional it was.

We all survived to tell the story. I thank the universe for all the people that were sent to me to help me find my way through these emotions.

I am grateful I allowed myself to deal with the things that held me back. Anxiety is manageable with the right tools. EFT has been my tool.

I am learning to listen to my gut. I am tuned into the fleeting messages that arrive. While I used to ignore these thoughts before, I now understand they are important messages and answers. I can hear, see, and feel them now. Practice makes perfect.

At my last visit to the dermatologist to seek treatment for

my ongoing battle with Licken Plantus, he said "You need to figure out what is eating you up."

What emotion is eating me up? Who is eating me up? When did this start? What happen just before my symptoms started showing up?

Thinking about these questions, I remembered it was after my Dad's death in 2007, two months before my son's wedding.

That certainly played a big role in what has been eating me up. With these issues on my mind, I was overwhelmed and exhausted to say the least.

Now that I know where it started I can let go of all the grief and loss. The feeling of helplessness is not a good feeling.

Tapping on these feelings and releasing this pain, I can feel the transformation starting to happen in side my body.

For me, knowing is the key. Once I know I can let go of anything within minutes. I will continue to remind myself of that fact.

I am doing it now, as I feel a warm breeze softly blowing across my face. Gently healing me from the all the loss and grief. I take a few deep breath and release more blocked energy. I continue tapping on all points to let all of that go. It was an extremely difficult time in my life.

Dad was the last parent to pass away. He was the provider, the head of the family. He was ninety-six years old, wise, accepting, generous and also a people pleaser in many ways. He was providing up to his very last day.

He had his son who struggled with his own issues living

with him, along with his grandson, partner and three children. He provided a roof over their heads, utilities, and food. They were often borrowing his truck. He had an incredible ability to adapt while keeping to his schedule.

I used to want to be like him, I now realize this is not who I want to be anymore. I want to be myself, living my truth and creating my own life.

Not only was I grieving the loss of Dad, I was dealing with the settling of the estate as co-executor, which created a lot of emotional distress.

I played the role of peacemaker again; it became a weekly job for me. My people-pleaser, bend-over-backwards skills can be useful in some situations, I guess.

Everyone wanted something different, a different idea of how it should be done. As a whole we did very well to complete every detail. When it came time to do things, I would hear, "Why can't you just do that?" Or "Can't your kids do that?" Or "I don't have time."

I accepted it all with one thought at the core: what would Mom and Dad want me to do? I know they wanted it to be done fairly and equally for each child.

I felt for a moment what Mom and Dad endured with each of us kids and our different personalities. I was seeing from a different perspective, understanding why my parents did what they did at times.

I was quick to realize, if this is to be, it will be up to me to do what needs to be done to finally put this to rest. I accepted that I would figure out what ever needed to be done.

Along with dealing with estate issues and everything I had on my own plate at the time with my own family issues. I felt overwhelmed and helpless.

I heard a lot about accepting and acceptance. How? Was I to accept what I was going through? How was I to accept all the people living in Dad's house? How could I accept things that were out of my control?

Then there was the Realtor hounding me to have the house that, all these people were living in clean for showings. How was I to accept all these changes?

Letting go was not in the cards..... I could not let go nor could I drop the ball on any of the things Dad expected from me. So I put one foot in front of the other each day, muzzling my pain and exhaustion. I knew without a doubt I would get the job done.

My husband and I left no stone unturned when it came to any issues in our family. I didn't realize how much this was eating away at our whole family, and kept pushing it down, which only added to my anxiety. I never thought of myself or how it was affecting me. I needed to be there for everyone no matter what it was. That was my belief, my conviction.

Today I recognize what I was doing to myself. I just realized sitting here in this beautiful setting that I created this pain by not understanding all the harm I was doing to myself.

A thought pops up in my head: all I have to do is help

myself. That sounds almost too easy. What about all these people I want to save?

All you have to do is save yourself. As they say in the airplane, put on your own oxygen mask before helping someone else with theirs.

Light Bulb Moment!

Well, that is a different perspective.

Another thought crosses my mind about Mom. She hung me when I was born.....like a chicken handing from a clothes line....What? Was I the chicken? Am I the chicken?

My Vision.... I was hung just high enough to keep me from the other chickens. She wanted to keep me from the pecking of the other chickens.

She hung me just high enough that no one could get to me with the secret. I knew that I had been chicken to look at the root of my problems.

I think to myself, a chicken. I could see I was still hanging on the line. I was observing the chicken. I could see its feet were not far from the ground. I asked the chicken what it had to tell me. What did I benefit from being a chicken?

The reply surprised me. It lays the golden egg. I felt my energy shift. If I was the chicken, I had the golden egg.

I had the power to let go of that image and put my feet flat on the ground, which I immediately did. The chicken was gone as my feet touched the ground.

I was grounded, I saw this dark haired, blue-eyed women. She was wearing a leather vest and shorts. I looked at her in disbelief, thinking, "You are so beautiful." I realized that she was me, my next though surprised me.

I am so much more than that vision. I see the power of my inner self. I see myself holding the golden egg, growing into my true self, the person I have become, filled with power. I am creating love, joy, and peace.

All my life I have be scared to death of chickens and all kinds of birds really. Wow... I see the connection.

Mom always liked birds. Even though she knew of my fear she bought a canary as a pet. She would tell me there was nothing to fear, since the bird was in a cage.

Then she gave me the job to clean the cage. I did it because she assured me it was easy, that all I had to do was pull out the tray, lay down new paper and put it back in, and fill the water tray while I was at it.

She also bought me bird pictures as well as bird ornaments. It did not sit well with me, yet I pushed down the feeling, not showing her it upset me.

I did not fight with Mom. I honored and supported her any way I could while she was alive.

However, after her death I began having nightmares. I would be so angry at her, fighting about all the cleaning she wanted me to do, it was no different than my real life. Yet in my nightmares, I fought her, screamed at her, and called her lazy.

As I was screaming at the top of my lungs, she would be waving birds in my face. I had this nightmare often.

During one of my first few sessions learning how EFT worked, my coach decided to bundle all my fear and release it. We never talked about birds, yet my fear of birds was also removed that day, which stopped the bird nightmares.

The cleaning and fighting dream continues. I even cleaned houses for a long time, bringing in a more negative association. I was unknowingly creating more pain so things could keep eating away at me. I was always complaining my way through it.

My emotions were swirling at this stage of my morning meditation and EFT.

I continued to tap. Even though I am carrying so much anger, and I am holding it in my stomach, I accept myself anyway. Even though I am carrying all of this anger, I see red, I accept myself anyway. I am so sick and tired of holding all this anger, making myself feel sick. I feel like I am stuck in a place I don't like.

What if I could change this? What if I could let go of even a little bit of this anger? I would like that. I hate where I am; it makes me feel overwhelmed, I can't think straight.

Tapping through these thoughts enabled the stuck energy to shift more.

The words "what if" are amazing and powerful. Somehow, they immediately cause you to shift your energy. What if I could let go of all this anger? What if it worked similar to my fear of birds, which I was able to overcome? What if...things I don't even realize I am angry at could just vanish as I release this anger?

It is a lifetime of anger at my mother, I guess. What would my life look like if I let it go? What would I do with all the space I could create by releasing this stuck anger?

Wow! There is a lot of it. How much could I create? First of all, I could have time and space to create my book, which is really important to me. My granddaughter is the most adorable little soul; I could spend more time with her.

Image if I let go of this anger, how that will that change all my relationships with my children and my husband?

I choose to let go of all this stuck energy I call anger. I do not want to pass any of this to my granddaughter, nor do I want anger to affect any of my relationships. I know I can feel the energy of other people, good or bad. I want mine to be good.

What if ....this is the one thing I have control over? What if.....I take back my power? Why did I give it to my mother in the first place? Why would any of us give it to anyone?

Energy has been shifting and another thought crosses my mind. Silly me, I don't want to be like this. This is hurting me. I deeply and complete love and accept myself.

I am free of all the pended up anger that I put there and carried around for forty-some years. I release it now. I chose to move forward free of any hurt, anger or negative memories of Mom and Dad, Mac or anyone who has ever came to my mind as a negative thought.

It Came as a Question

Are you eating away at yourself?

Are you allowing this anger to live in your body?

Are you feeding it with your thoughts?

This is my least favorite part...

Admitting to myself, YES I AM!

Tap, Tap, Tap,

I stood up, alone, free of all that past negativity. My immune system reset to exactly the right place. I felt calm and at peace, knowing exactly what I would do next.

FINISH MY BOOK!

ABOUT THE EDITOR

Ruqaya Ahmed graduated with the Bachelor's Degree (summa am laude) in English from York University, where she also studied Professional Writing. She lives with her husband and son, working as a freelance copyeditor.

ABOUT THE AUTHOR

Elaine Cox was born in 1956. She and her husband just celebrated their forty first Wedding Anniversary. Together they raised 3 children and welcomed their first grandchild this past year.

Her love to learn allowed her to earn the following Diploma's Early Childhood, Teacher Assistant, and Child Psychology.

Personal growth has been at the center of her being. Reading everything she could get her hands and attending workshops was her passion.

She was introduced to EFT in 2009. Elaine completed the Gary Craig EFT Course. This experience opened her up to teaching and helping others as an EFT coach.

Experiencing and seeing the results and benefits of EFT for herself and her clients, she felt compelled to reach more individuals.

Elaine talks of her strong desire to write books, how she believes, she is being called to reach people all over the world.

Her journey with EFT has healed her past, creating many opportunity for a bright, healthy happy future.

Printed in the United States
By Bookmasters